Marching

I CAN READ ABOUT

CREATURES OF THE NIGHT

Written by David Cutts

Illustrated by Jean Chandler

Troll Associates

Library of Congress Catalog Card Number: 78-68468
ISBN 0-89375-202-9

10 9 8 7 6 5 4 3 2

What a beautiful day!
The sun is shining. Birds are singing.
Bees are buzzing. Butterflies fly from
flower to flower. Chipmunks scamper for
nuts and seeds. All day long, the
animals of the day are busy.

Now the sun has dipped below the trees. Darkness is falling on the fields and forests. The animals of the daytime have settled down for the night.

The moon is out, and the
stars are twinkling. The animals
of the daytime are silent.
But if you listen closely, you
can hear something else.
Shhh...listen!

Can you hear the creatures
of the night?
Some of them move around on the
ground. Others climb about in the
trees. Still others fly through the
air.
    Can you hear them? Do you see them?

Fireflies, or lightning bugs, fly around looking for mates. Special chemicals mix inside their bodies as they fly. The chemicals make a light inside the lightning bug. This is why fireflies are easy to see when it is dark.

Moths are easy to see when
they fly near bright lights. Moths
are related to butterflies. But when
the sun goes down and the butterflies
go to sleep, the moths fly about,
searching for flowers.

Each moth sips the nectar through a long tube that works like a straw. When the tube is not being used, it is curled up like a spring.

There are thousands of kinds of moths. Some are painted green, gold, pink, or even blue. Some of these moths do not taste good. Their bright colors warn their enemies not to eat them. So they do not have to hide.

But many moths would make tasty
dinners for the spiders or frogs or
lizards that are out looking for a meal.
So these moths often have dull colors
to help them hide in the night.

Some of the strangest creatures
of the night are bats. Bats are the only
animals in the world that have wings and fur.
Many animals have fur, but they do not have wings.

Many insects have wings, but they do not have fur.
And birds have wings, but they have feathers
instead of fur.

A bat's wings are made of thin skin. This *membrane,* or thin skin, stretches between the bones of the fingers and the legs. Bats also have a tail membrane. It stretches from one leg to the other.

Bats use the claws on their feet
to hang upside down. That's how they sleep
all through the day. Some sleep in caves.
Others sleep in trees or in empty
buildings. Sometimes bats sleep
in attics. At night, they fly
outside to hunt for food.

Most bats eat insects that
fly at night—like mosquitoes and
moths and gnats. They catch their
food in the air. A bat uses its wings
like a broom. It sweeps an insect
into its tail membrane. Then it
bends its head down and eats the insect.

To take a drink, a bat flies low
over a pond or lake. It skims the surface
of the water with its lower jaw.

Bats have tiny eyes, and poor eyesight.
But their large ears help them to hear very well.

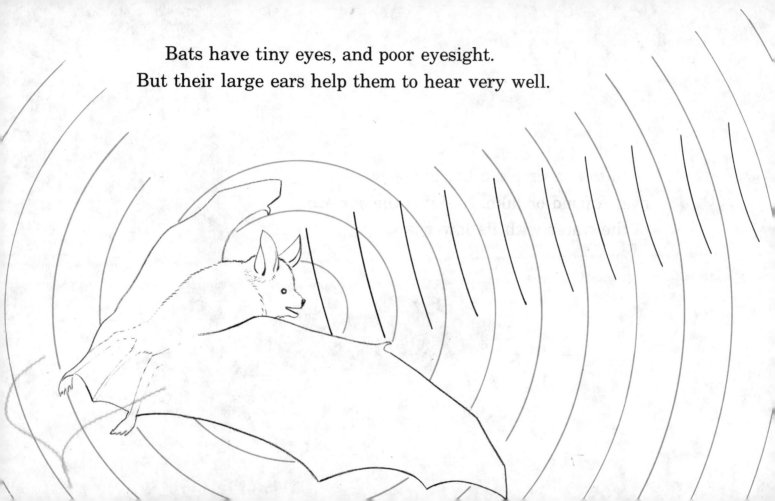

When a bat flies, it makes
special sounds. People cannot hear
these sounds, but the bat can. Each sound
bounces off the flying insect, and an echo
comes back. The bat hears the echoes and knows
exactly where the insect is.
That's why bats are such good flyers.
They can find their way around on the darkest nights,
without bumping into anything.

Many animals of the night
have large ears, so they can hear
what they do not see. Mice cannot
see well, but they have large ears
and excellent hearing. They also have
long whiskers that help them feel their
way around as they search for food.

In fields and forests,
most mice eat seeds, grain, plant stems,
and roots. They dig down into the ground
to build their nests. Then they line
them with soft grass.

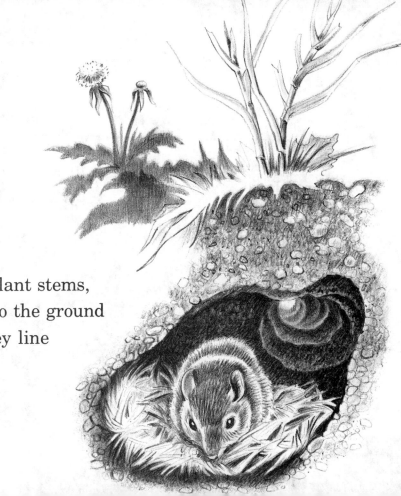

The grasshopper mouse lives on the
desert or prairie. It makes its home
in an old burrow that may have been dug
by a prairie dog or a gopher.

Grasshopper mice like to eat animals instead of plants. They search for worms and scorpions, and other small creatures of the night. But they get their name from their favorite food—grasshoppers!

Many other animals that live on the desert and prairie are creatures of the night. It is too hot during the day to move around much. So pocket mice and kangaroo rats curl up in their cool bedrooms below the ground.

Here and there a ground squirrel pokes its head up out of its burrow. Sleepy lizards and snakes move from the sun into the shade, where it is cooler.

But at night, the desert comes alive. A pocket mouse steals out, looking for seeds. Soon the fur-lined pockets on the sides of its neck are full, so it scampers down to its underground storeroom. Kangaroo rats hop around on their hind legs—just like tiny kangaroos. When they have to, they can jump as far as fourteen feet in one hop!

Ground squirrels are out, gathering nuts and grain. They also chase after insects and mice. But when a coyote comes looking for a meal, the ground squirrels hurry into their homes. There they are safe from coyotes, and from foxes and owls—but not from snakes and badgers.

Badgers can dig down into the burrows of ground squirrels, pocket mice, and kangaroo rats. A badger has large strong claws on its front feet, so it can dig very quickly.

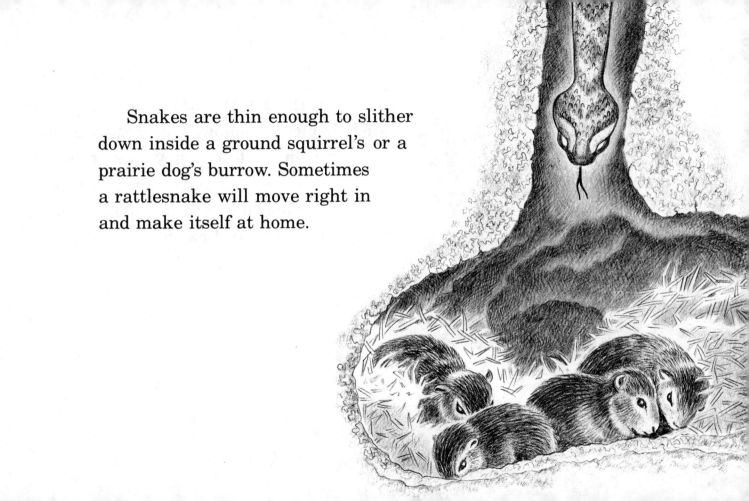

Snakes are thin enough to slither
down inside a ground squirrel's or a
prairie dog's burrow. Sometimes
a rattlesnake will move right in
and make itself at home.

In the desert, owls sometimes make
their homes in hollowed-out cactus plants.
But in the forest they roost, or settle
down to rest, in trees.
Their big eyes can spot a mouse,
rabbit, or squirrel on the darkest night.

Then the owl swoops down and grabs its prey in its sharp *talons,* or claws. Back in its nest, it uses its curved beak for ripping and tearing. Owls gulp down their prey—feathers, fur, bones and all.

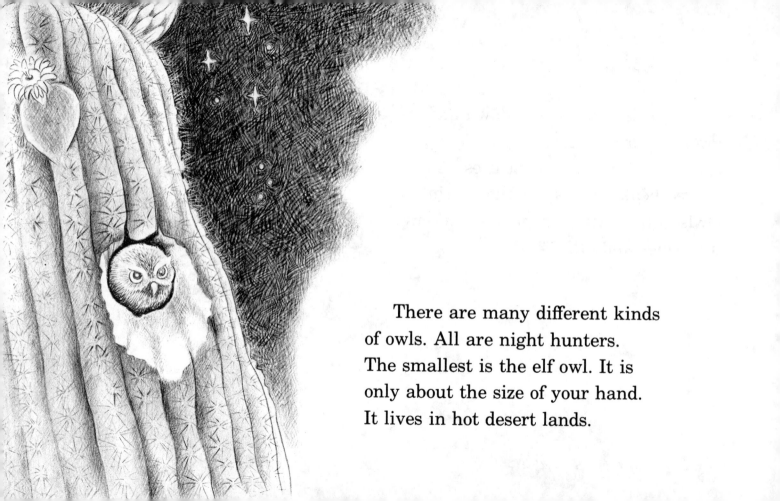

There are many different kinds
of owls. All are night hunters.
The smallest is the elf owl. It is
only about the size of your hand.
It lives in hot desert lands.

The largest is the gray owl.
It can stretch out its wings
farther than you can stretch
your arms. It lives in the
forests of Alaska and Canada.

Did you ever try to fool someone by "playing possum"?
We get this name from a creature of the night called the opossum.

When the opossum is afraid, it sometimes rolls over and pretends to be dead. Then, when its enemy looks the other way, it climbs a tree to get away. It can even hang by its tail, like a monkey.

An opossum mother keeps her babies
with her all the time. When they are
born, they are very tiny and helpless.
They stay in their mother's pouch.
Later, they ride on her back.
Finally, they are strong enough
to walk and climb and search for
food. "Possums" eat fruit, nuts,
and tender plants.

Is this a walking pincushion?
A porcupine's body is covered with long, stiff quills.
Each quill has tiny sharp hooks on the end.
Sometimes a coyote or wolf or lynx
gets too close. Then it gets
stuck with the porcupine's
quills.

Porcupines sleep during the day
in holes in the ground, or between rocks.
At night, they climb into evergreen trees
to eat the tender bark.

Skunks eat different kinds of food.
They roam through the woodlands at night,
looking for insects, fruit, small furry animals, eggs,
nuts, and grass. Their favorite food is caterpillars.

Sometimes a skunk is annoyed by
someone or something. When this happens,
the skunk raises its tail. Then it stamps
its front feet. If this warning is ignored,
the skunk lets out a foul smell.
That's enough to chase
anyone away!

Beavers cannot protect themselves with strong
odors or sharp quills or by playing possum. Instead,
they build special houses that keep them safe from their
enemies. All night long, they are working and building.
Beavers use their sharp teeth to gnaw through trees.

Then they build a dam to make a pond.
In the middle of the pond, they build a lodge or house.
It has an underwater entrance, to keep visitors out.
But the beavers can swim in and out easily. With their
webbed feet and flat tails, they are at home in the water.

Crash. Bang. Who's out there by the garbage can?
It's the midnight thief! The clever raccoon uses
its paws just like hands. It quickly learns to
solve problems...like how to open a garbage can
to find scraps of food.

A mother raccoon teaches her babies how to find worms, insects, turtle eggs, and berries. She shows them how to catch tadpoles, fish, frogs and salamanders. But raccoons are very curious. That's why they sometimes get into midnight mischief when people build houses near the woods.

When the sun comes up, the raccoons are gone. All the creatures of the night seem to have vanished. And by the time you wake up, they are already sound asleep for another day.

But when darkness comes again,
the animals of the night will be back…
creeping and climbing, swooping and flying.
They will be slithering and scurrying and
snooping around, looking for something to eat.
So if you hear a sound in the middle
of the night, take a peek out of your window.

Who knows what fascinating creatures are out there.